KNOWING GOD IN THE QUIET

EJIRO OBAYOMI

Contents

To my incredible husband, Busola Iseoluwa Obayomi
Your unwavering support, quiet strength, and constant belief in me
have carried me through every chapter of my life journey.
Thank you for always standing beside me, encouraging me, and loving
me through it all.
This book is as much yours as it is mine.

Chapter One

Introduction

In December 2022, the Lord spoke words to me that began a journey I did not expect, one that would change everything. His message was simple and clear, yet it stirred something deep within me, something I could not ignore:

"I died for so much more than what you have been living for."

Those words echoed through me, louder than anything I had ever heard before. As someone who had walked with Jesus for as long as I could remember, I thought I understood what it meant to follow Him. I believed in His sacrifice, trusted His promises, and shaped my life around what I knew of Him. But those words shook me to my core. They revealed something I did not realize had settled into my heart—a spiritual complacency. I had settled into a safe and comfortable version of faith, unaware I was missing the very life Jesus died to give me.

This realization unraveled a faith built around comfort and familiarity and began something raw, real, and deeply refining. This journey has not been easy. It has pulled me out of my assumptions, challenged my beliefs, and revealed how much I still have to learn. With every step, Holy Spirit has drawn me closer to truth, closer to conviction, and closer to the heart of God.

I began to see scripture differently. Verses I had read countless times opened up in new ways. Holy Spirit began revealing insights I never would have reached on my own. Soon I recognized this journey was bigger than my own experiences. It was about the call resting on all of us who follow Jesus—to live a life that reflects His sacrifice. To live for more.

This book is a collection of truths revealed to me throughout this process. These truths are incomplete, and I have far to go in my learning. Yet what I share here has been tested in quiet places, through prayer, surrender, and the slow and steady work of transformation. These reflections are for anyone who senses there is more to their faith than what they have been living.

I believe this book is as much for me as it is for you. Writing it is part of my own growth, a step of obedience responding to what God is doing in me. If it draws you closer to Him, if it awakens something in you, then it has accomplished what it was meant to do.

Chapter Two

The Call of God

During His time on earth, Jesus was constantly surrounded by people. Crowds pressed in, needs overflowed, and voices called out. Wherever He went, He drew attention. People had heard of His miracles, His teachings, and His power, and they pleaded for Him to visit their towns, their homes, their lives.

Yet through all of this, Jesus remained focused. He did not move based on popularity, pressure, or urgency. He moved with purpose.

In *Mark 1:37–38*, we see His disciples searching for Him after a time of solitude. When they find Him, they exclaim:

"Everyone is looking for you!"

Jesus responds with clarity:

"Let us go into the next towns, that I may preach there also, because for this purpose I have come."

This moment reveals something essential about the nature of God's call. Jesus did not react to demand. He followed mission. He understood His purpose and refused to let the clamor of the crowd pull Him away from it.

Even as a child, Jesus showed awareness of His Father's calling. In *Luke 2:46–52*, we find twelve-year-old Jesus sitting among temple teachers, asking questions and giving answers. When His parents locate Him, He says:

"Did you not know that I must be about My Father's business?"

This was not defiance. It was clarity. Jesus understood His identity and purpose.

We may be tempted to think this kind of clarity belonged only to Jesus. Yet throughout scripture, we see that God often reveals purpose early in the lives of those He chooses.

- Joseph received dreams at seventeen.

- Samuel heard God's voice as a child in the temple.

- David was anointed while he was still tending sheep.

- Jeremiah was called before birth.

- Daniel, Gideon, Timothy—all received their call in youth.

God's purpose is not delayed by age or readiness. It follows His timing and intention. Often, it begins before we can fully grasp it.

I have also sensed God's hand on my life from a young age. When I turned eighteen, my pastor asked me to lead the church choir. Though I was younger than those around me, I recognized the grace of God covering every step. From age eighteen to twenty-three, I led worship. During that time, I heard the Lord speak words I thought I understood:

"You were created to worship."

I held on to those words. I wrote them down. I believed they meant singing. I saw worship as music and music as my calling. I lived as a vocalist and leader, believing I had found my purpose.

But God was reaching deeper.

In the midst of ministry and music, a new message began to stir:

"Separate yourself from the noise so you can hear Me."

At first, I was unsure what to do with it. I wrote it down and prayed. Over time, I came to understand that God was calling me beyond activity. He was inviting me into presence.

God's call begins with quiet. Not with withdrawal from people, but from the constant distractions that keep us from hearing. His voice often comes without drama. It rises gently. It whispers through motion. It lingers until we stop long enough to notice.

To respond, we must be willing to pause. To make room. To release our assumptions about purpose so we can receive what God is really saying.

Reflection

Ask yourself:

1. Have I confused my role with my calling?

2. What noise in my life may be keeping me from hearing God clearly?

3. Am I willing to pause—not to disconnect, but to truly listen?

Scripture Meditation

Take time to read and reflect on each of these verses. Invite the Holy Spirit to speak to you through them.

- **Mark 1:37–38** — *"Everyone is looking for You. But He said to them, 'Let us go into the next towns, that I may preach there also, because for this purpose I have come.'"*

- **Luke 2:49** — *"Did you not know that I must be about My Father's business?"*

- **1 Timothy 4:12** — *"Let no one despise your youth, but be an example to the believers in word, in conduct, in love, in spirit, in faith, in purity."*

Chapter Three

Known Before Formed

"Before I formed you in the womb, I knew you."—Je-
remiah 1:5

These words spoken to the prophet Jeremiah by God, were not just words, they carried revelation. The Lord God in His statement to Jeremiah revealed a deep truth about what happens during creation. God did not simply know of Jeremiah's existence; He knew him because Jeremiah was already in Him.

Before Jeremiah had a body, a voice, or a name on earth, he lived in the heart of God. His spirit existed in eternity, and at the appointed time, God gave him a physical form. This pattern of creation did not begin with Jeremiah. It reflects how God forms each of us.

When God created Adam, He did not begin with dust. He began with Himself. Adam's spirit came from within God. The dust became the vessel that carried the life God already knew. The same is true for us. We are spirit before anything else. Our bodies serve as temporary dwellings, but who we truly are lives in the spirit.

This truth became evident in the moments following the fall.

When Adam sinned, something shifted in the unseen realm.

In *Genesis 3:9*, God walked through the garden and called out:

"Adam, where are you?"

God was not looking for Adam's location. He already knew where his body stood. He was searching for the spirit of the one He had always communed with. That connection had been interrupted. The familiar closeness had been replaced with distance. The spirit that once lived in God's presence was now hidden.

This was not a question of confusion. It was a cry from the depths of love:

"Adam, I no longer find you where you belong."

From that moment forward, everything God put into motion was meant to bring humanity back to that original place of unity. A return to life in Him. A return to full communion; spirit living in Spirit. Fully alive. Fully known. Fully at home in God.

Jesus confirmed this truth when He said in *John 15:5*:

"Apart from Me, you can do nothing."

Disconnection from God brings spiritual death. We may continue to function outwardly, speak, plan, and succeed by earthly standards, yet without connection to Him, we are missing the very life we were created for. In Jesus, the way back has been revealed.

We were created to draw life from the Spirit. We were created to dwell in the presence of God.

We are spiritual beings, given physical bodies to navigate this world. But our true design points us back to abiding in Him.

This is why Jesus said:

"God is Spirit, and those who worship Him must worship in spirit and truth."(John 4:24)

The presence of God is accessed through the spirit. Our natural efforts, no matter how sincere, cannot reach Him without that spiritual connection.

Proverbs 20:27 says:

"The spirit of a man is the lamp of the Lord."

This is where God looks. This is the place He searches. And when sin clouds that light, the voice of God calls out once more:

"Where are you?"

The invitation to return continues till today. Through Jesus, what was once separated has been rejoined. The way is open again.

We were formed to live in God. And in Christ, we can.

Reflection

Ask yourself:

1. Am I living with awareness of my spirit, or only responding to my body and emotions?

2. Where have I drifted from the truth of my spiritual identity in God?

3. Can I sense God asking me, "Where are you?" and am I ready to draw near again?

Scripture Meditation

Take time to read and reflect on each of these verses. Invite the Holy Spirit to speak to you through them.

- **Jeremiah 1:5** — *"Before I formed you in the womb I knew you; before you were born I sanctified you."*

- **Genesis 3:9** — *"Adam, where are you?"*

- **John 15:5** — *"Apart from Me you can do nothing."*

- **John 4:24** — *"God is Spirit, and those who worship Him must worship in spirit and truth."*

- **Proverbs 20:27** — *"The spirit of a man is the lamp of the Lord, searching all the inner depths of his heart."*

Chapter Four

The Power of Words

I n the Kingdom of God, words are never just sounds or expressions. They carry power. Words create. Words destroy. They build, uproot, give life, and bring things down. Everything that moves in the Kingdom flows through the vehicle of the spoken word.

In the natural realm, physical actions create visible results. In the spiritual realm, change begins with what is spoken. Both life and destruction take root in the unseen through words. This is why the enemy works so persistently to silence believers, especially in prayer. In the Kingdom of God, it is the spoken word that carries authority.

When God called the prophet Jeremiah, He revealed this truth with clarity. In *Jeremiah 1:9–10*, it says:

"Then the Lord put forth His hand and touched my mouth, and the Lord said to me: 'Behold, I have put My words in your mouth. See, I have this day set you over the nations and over the kingdoms, to root out and to pull down, to destroy and to throw down, to build and to plant.'"

The first thing God did was touch Jeremiah's mouth.

This was not a symbolic gesture. It was a strategic move. God was preparing Jeremiah for a spiritual assignment that would require influence in the unseen world. That influence would come through the spoken word.

God did not give Jeremiah a sword or supplies. He gave him His words. And those words held the power to shift nations and destroy strongholds. Jeremiah's role was to speak them.

It is not surprising, then, that Jesus is described as the Word of God. *John 1:1* says:

"In the beginning was the Word, and the Word was with God, and the Word was God."

And *verse 3* continues:

"All things were made through Him, and without Him nothing was made that was made."

Jesus—the living Word—took on flesh and walked the earth. The One through whom all things were created entered time and space. Although He lived among men, His most powerful acts were not physical. He healed through words. He cast out demons through words. He declared truth through words.

This is how He could say, "The Kingdom of God has come near." He was the Word of God, walking in human form. His very presence announced the arrival of the Kingdom.

This same truth explains why spoken faith-filled prayer faces such intense resistance. The enemy understands the power of words spoken in alignment with God. He knows what happens when a believer speaks with boldness and faith. Heaven responds. Darkness is disrupted.

Prayer is not a passing thought. It is a spiritual act that carries weight.

In the Kingdom of God, words are the force that brings heaven into the earth.

God creates through speech.

Jesus, the eternal Word, holds all things together by what He speaks. And now, His people are called to speak with that same understanding.

Speak with faith. Declare the truth. Pray with authority. Prayers are not empty expressions. They are how heaven advances.

Reflection

Ask yourself:

1. Do I speak with the authority God has given me, or have I grown quiet when I was meant to pray?

2. What would change in my life if I truly believed my words, when aligned with God's Word, could shape the world around me?

Scripture Meditation

Take time to read and reflect on each of these verses. Invite the Holy Spirit to speak to you through them.

- **Jeremiah 1:9** — *"Then the Lord put forth His hand and touched my mouth, and the Lord said to me: 'Behold, I have put My words in your mouth.'"*

- **John 1:1, 3** — *"In the beginning was the Word, and the Word was with God, and the Word was God... All things were made through Him, and without Him nothing was made that was made."*

- **Proverbs 18:21** — *"Death and life are in the power of the tongue, and those who love it will eat its fruit."*

Chapter Five

The Word That Fills

*"Man shall not live by bread alone, but by every word
that proceeds from the mouth of God."— Matthew 4:4*

These words from Jesus were an invitation to real life, the kind of life that cannot be sustained by food, achievement, or daily routines. This life is sustained by the Word. It is fueled by the presence of God.

In *John 1:1*, we read:

"In the beginning was the Word, and the Word was with God, and the Word was God."

Jesus is not simply a messenger delivering truth. He is the Word Himself. He stepped into human form and lived among us. He did not only speak divine truth, He is truth. His life revealed what the Word looks like when it takes on flesh.

Then He declared something even more personal:

"I am the bread of life."— John 6:35

Jesus, who is the Word, is also the Bread. Just as bread nourishes the body, the Word nourishes the spirit. His invitation is not only to hear Him or follow Him, but to feed on Him—to take Him in as our source of life.

Jesus said:

"He who eats My flesh and drinks My blood abides in Me, and I in him."— John 6:56

This kind of language was difficult for many to accept. But Jesus was pointing to a spiritual reality. His flesh and blood represent all that He is; His life, His truth, His sacrifice, and His presence. To eat and drink is to receive Him deeply, to commune with Him continually, to abide.

This is how we are filled.

The world teaches us to eat for strength, to consume for satisfaction, and to fill our lives with noise, speed, and sensation. But none of it nourishes the spirit. None of it satisfies the soul.

Jesus said:

"My flesh is food indeed, and My blood is drink indeed."— John 6:55

Only He can truly sustain us. Only the Word can satisfy the hunger that runs deeper than the body. The Word of God is not an accessory to our lives. It is our life. The more we feed on it, the more alive we become. We become clearer in purpose, stronger in spirit, more grounded in truth.

Spiritual hunger is not solved by more activity or greater ambition. It is satisfied in one way: through consistent, personal communion with Jesus, the Bread of Life.

This is why we cannot treat the Word as an obligation or a task. It is not a box to check. It is a table to sit at. The Word is nourishment. It fills us with wisdom. It revives what feels dry. It awakens what has gone numb. It reminds us of who we are, and who He is.

To live fully, we must feast on Jesus daily, moment by moment. We need His Word like we need breath. Our bodies are sustained by physical food. Our spirits are sustained by Him.

Reflection

Ask Yourself:

1. What am I feeding my soul with?

2. Am I filling up on the noise and urgency of the world—or on the quiet, life-giving presence of Jesus?

3. Are my daily rhythms leaving space to be fed by the Word?

4. What would it look like to treat God's Word as my daily meal, not a religious task?

Scripture Meditation

Take time to read and reflect on each of these verses. Invite the Holy Spirit to speak to you through them.

- **John 6:35** — *"Jesus said to them, 'I am the bread of life. Whoever comes to me shall not hunger, and whoever believes in me shall never thirst.'"*

- **Matthew 4:4** — *"Man shall not live by bread alone, but by every word that proceeds from the mouth of God."*

- **John 6:56** — *"He who eats My flesh and drinks My blood abides in Me, and I in him."*

Chapter Six

To Know and To Be Known

Jesus walked the earth fully aware of who He was. Though He lived in a human body, a temporary vessel, He never lost sight of His eternal identity. He knew He was Spirit dwelling in a physical world. He knew His origin, His assignment, and His destination.

Jesus never moved from a place of confusion or insecurity. He never questioned His worth, His authority, or His purpose. *John 13:3–4* gives us a glimpse into that inner confidence:

"Jesus, knowing that the Father had given all things into His hands, and that He had come from God and was going to God, rose from supper... and began to wash the disciples' feet."

Even in the act of serving, Jesus moved from a deep assurance. He was not trying to prove anything. He was revealing something. He lived with the full knowledge of who He was.

His spiritual vision was clear. His mission was to help others see with the same clarity. He came to open the eyes of those who lived in darkness—both spiritually and physically.

In *Luke 4:18*, Jesus declared:

"The Spirit of the Lord is upon Me, because He has anointed Me to preach the gospel to the poor; He has sent Me to heal the brokenhearted, to proclaim liberty to the captives and recovery of sight to the blind..."

This declaration extended far beyond physical healing. Jesus came to awaken people to their true identity in God. He came to restore awareness of their origin, their belonging, and their spiritual position.

Jesus Himself was born into humble conditions. He grew up in Nazareth, the son of a carpenter. There was no outward glory in His surroundings. Yet He never allowed His birthplace or social standing to define Him. He lived from the Spirit, not from circumstance. And He longed to give others that same clarity of vision.

Throughout human history, the battle for identity has always been at the center. When Adam and Eve ate from the tree of the knowledge of good and evil, they did more than disobey. They lost their sense of identity. Their eyes were opened to sin but closed to truth. In that moment, humanity lost sight. From then on, every person has entered the world unaware of who they are apart from Christ.

This is why Jesus came. He came to restore sight, to reawaken us to the knowledge of God and who we are in Him. To lead us back to truth.

Jesus is the Light of the world. Only He can remove the darkness and help us see again. Without Him, we cannot understand our purpose. We cannot see where we are going. We cannot recognize the One who made us.

But in Christ, our vision is restored. In Christ, we come back to knowing, and in that knowing, we also discover that we are fully known.

Reflection

Ask yourself:

1. Am I living from who I truly am, or only from what I observe in the natural?

2. What areas of my identity are still shaped by misunderstanding or lack of truth?

3. Have I invited the Light of Christ to renew my spiritual sight?

Scripture Meditation

Take time to read and reflect on each of these verses. Invite the Holy Spirit to speak to you through them.

- **Luke 4:18** — *"The Spirit of the LORD is upon Me, because He has anointed Me... to proclaim liberty to the captives and recovery of sight to the blind."*

- **John 13:3** — *"Jesus, knowing that the Father had given all things into His hands, and that He had come from God and was going to God..."*

- **John 8:12** — *"I am the Light of the world. He who follows Me shall not walk in darkness but have the light of life."*

- **1 Corinthians 13:12** — *"For now we see in a mirror, dimly, but then face to face. Now I know in part, but then I shall know just as I also am known."*

Chapter Seven

Where Light Dwells

"God is light, and in Him is no darkness at all."— *1 John 1:5*

From the very beginning, scripture tells us that God is light. This does not mean He simply radiates light or brings it forth. He is light itself. In Him, there is no shadow, no deception, and no impurity. His light is perfect, holy, and pure.

That is why it may seem curious when we read in *Genesis 1:3*:

"Then God said, 'Let there be light'; and there was light."

If God is light, and His presence fills all things, why would He need to speak light into being? Why didn't His own glory illuminate the earth from the beginning, as it does in the new creation described in *Revelation 21:23*?

The answer appears in the verse just before:

"...And darkness was on the face of the deep."— *Genesis 1:2*

This darkness represented more than the absence of physical light; this was spiritual darkness.

Long before humanity entered the scene, the earth had been touched by evil, because of the angelic rebellion and the punished given to them, to be cast down to the earth. The darkness present at creation was the deep darkness of rebellion and corruption.

Still, God moved. He spoke light into the darkness.

From the first moments of creation, God set in motion a plan to confront and overcome darkness. His purpose was to remove it fully. Yet there is a deeper truth in this passage: while God can shine into darkness, He will not dwell in it. His presence rests where there is holiness. His glory resides in purity.

This is why God did not immediately fill the earth with His glory. The earth was already filled with rebellion. Instead, He spoke: *"Let there be light."* In that declaration, He revealed His divine intention. Darkness was to be pushed out by the power of His Word. And from that moment, creation began to take shape.

The plan did not stop there.

God formed humanity in His own image. He created man to reflect Him, to carry His light into the world. Just as Jesus would later say, *"I am the Light of the world,"* man was created to live in that light and reveal it to all of creation.

But man fell.

When sin entered humanity, the light within was dimmed. Sin had already touched the earth through the fall of the rebellious angels. But now, the vessels designed to hold God's light were affected from within.

Even so, God's plan did not stop.

From the beginning, His purpose was not only to forgive sin, but to remove its power entirely. His goal was to eliminate darkness altogether; to form a people and a place where His presence could remain, not temporarily, but forever.

We see the fulfillment of this vision in *Revelation 21:23*:

"The city had no need of the sun or of the moon to shine in it, for the glory of God illuminated it. The Lamb is its light."

This is the final picture: a redeemed people, cleansed by the blood of Jesus, hosting the presence of God without interruption or limit.

This is the reason Jesus came. This is the purpose of the cross. Not only to forgive sin, but to free us from it.

Through Christ, we become a place where light dwells. When we believe in Him, we are made new. Darkness no longer defines us. His light begins to live within us. And through us, that light reaches the world.

This is why He came. This is why He died.So we could walk and live in His light; free, clean, and filled with His glory.

Reflection

Ask yourself:

1. Am I living as someone created to reflect the light of God?

2. What would it look like to become a place where His glory remains—not temporarily, but fully?

Scripture Meditation

Take time to read and reflect on each of these verses. Invite the Holy Spirit to speak to you through them.

- **1 John 1:5** — *"God is light and in Him is no darkness at all."*

- **Genesis 1:3** — *"Then God said, 'Let there be light'; and there was light."*

- **Revelation 21:23** — *"The city had no need of the sun or of the moon to shine in it, for the glory of God illuminated it. The Lamb is its light."*

- **John 8:12** — *"I am the Light of the world. He who follows Me shall not walk in darkness but have the light of life."*

Chapter Eight

The Mystery of His Will

B efore the foundation of the world, God had already formed a plan. It was a divine mystery, hidden within Himself long before the earth was created, or mankind took its first breath.

In the beginning, God created the heavens and the sons of God, the angels. Over time, rebellion rose up among them. *Isaiah 14:12–15* gives us a glimpse into this, showing the fall of Lucifer, a created being who sought to lift himself above the One who formed him.

That rebellion, once limited to the heavens, soon entered the earth. The serpent, Satan, deceived Eve in the garden, and through disobedience, humanity joined the same rebellion that had already begun in the unseen realm (*Genesis 3*). From that moment forward, the enemy and the fallen sons of God were permitted to influence the earth, continuing their resistance against the will of God.

Yet God was never surprised. Before any of it unfolded, He had already crafted a response. The plan was hidden in Himself, veiled from plain view, and destined to be revealed in Jesus Christ.

That plan was never about patching up the old. It was about making something entirely new.

Paul writes in *2 Corinthians 5:17*:

"Therefore, if anyone is in Christ, he is a new creation."

This new creation is not a repaired version of what once was. It is completely transformed. Those who place their faith in Jesus are no longer defined by earthly origin or spiritual history; We are reborn, sanctified, and remade by the Spirit of God.

As new creations, we are given authority over every force of rebellion, both spiritual and earthly. *John 1:12* says:

"But as many as received Him, to them He gave the right to become children of God, to those who believe in His name."

This right is not earned. It is freely given by grace through faith.

To affirm this new identity, God places a seal within His people; Holy Spirit.

Ephesians 1:13–14 declares:

"You were sealed with the Holy Spirit of promise, who is the guarantee of our inheritance until the redemption of the purchased possession, to the praise of His glory."

Holy Spirit is our confirmation. He marks us as belonging to Christ. He is the evidence that we are joined to the New Creation.

Those who refuse Jesus remain outside this covenant. They do not carry His seal, and by choice, they remain separate. When Christ returns, He will gather those who are hidden in Him; those sealed by the Spirit. Others will face the judgment already written.

As Paul and Barnabas said in *Acts 13:46*:

"Since you reject it and do not consider yourselves worthy of eternal life, we now turn to the Gentiles."

Jesus bore the wrath meant for the disobedient. Both *Ephesians 5:6* and *Colossians 3:6* speak of this coming judgment. Yet at the cross,

Jesus took that punishment upon Himself. The work is already complete. Our only part is to believe, receive, and surrender.

Salvation is not earned. It is given to those who choose to received it.

Colossians 3:3 says:

"Your life is hidden with Christ in God."

This is our shelter. This is where we are made whole. This is where we are safe.

The mystery of God's will is no longer hidden. It has been revealed through Jesus.

The will of God is that through Jesus Christ, we receive grace. In Jesus, we find redemption. In Jesus, we are made new. In Jesus, we are restored back to our rightful place in God.

Paul writes in *Ephesians 2:8–9*:

"For by grace you have been saved through faith, and that not of yourselves; it is the gift of God, not of works, lest anyone should boast."

This is the gospel. God accomplished the plan while we were still lost. He completed the work while we were still distant. He loved us long before we turned toward Him.

This is grace. This is the mystery of His will, and in Christ, we are now part of it; but only if you make the decision to accept Him.

Reflection

Ask Yourself:

    1. Do I see myself as part of God's new creation, or am I still living as if I belong to the old?

    2. Where have I struggled to accept that salvation is a gift and not something I must earn?

    3. Am I living as someone sealed by the Spirit, secure in the One to whom I belong?

Scripture Meditation

Take time to read and reflect on each of these verses. Invite the Holy Spirit to speak to you through them.

- **2 Corinthians 5:17** — *"Therefore, if anyone is in Christ, he is a new creation; old things have passed away; behold, all things have become new."*

- **Ephesians 1:13–14** — *"Having believed, you were sealed with the Holy Spirit of promise, who is the guarantee of our inheritance until the redemption of the purchased possession."*

- **Ephesians 2:8** — *"For by grace you have been saved through faith, and that not of yourselves; it is the gift of God."*

Chapter Nine

Called Out & Set Apart

"Do not be conformed to this world, but be transformed by the renewing of your mind."— Romans 12:2

The enemy often avoids loud, obvious attacks. His strategy is more subtle, working through repetition, exposure, and slow influence. He trains us over time, not through force, but through the patterns of a world that does not know God.

Through what we watch, what we listen to, what we say, and even what we consume physically, our thoughts and habits can gradually shift. Without noticing, we begin to absorb values and lifestyles that do not reflect the heart of the Kingdom.

This is how conformity happens. Not all at once, but little by little. Not through dramatic choices, but through quiet compromise.

Eventually, identity grows faint. Conviction becomes dull. And the truth of who we are begins to slip from view.

But we are not of this world. We are citizens of Heaven, sons and daughters of the Kingdom of God. This is why the instruction in *Romans 12:2* matters so deeply:

"Do not be conformed to this world but be transformed by the renewing of your mind."

To be transformed is to be changed at the core. To live in the Kingdom requires a renewed mind, a mind shaped by truth, not trends. One filled with light, not shadows.

Renewing the mind does not happen automatically. It takes intention. It takes surrender. It happens through daily alignment with the Word of God.

We renew our minds by:

- Meditating on His Word until it reorders how we think

- Filtering what we take in, visually, audibly, physically through eating and emotionally

- Choosing to obey truth, even when it challenges comfort

Even small daily decisions can reflect a renewed mind:

- In what we say: *"Let your words be filled with grace, seasoned with salt, so they may bless the hearer."* (*Colossians 4:6*)

- In what we consume:What we watch, read, or scroll through is either feeding our spirit or weakening it.

- Even in what we eat and how we care for our bodies:God created our bodies as vessels for His glory, and honoring Him includes how we treat them.

Daniel understood this principle. In *Daniel 1:8*, we read:

"Daniel purposed in his heart that he would not defile himself with the portion of the king's delicacies."

His refusal was not only about the food. It was about devotion. Daniel chose restraint because he recognized that compromise would violate his identity. He belonged to God. His life was not his own. His body was consecrated for God's use.

In the same way, we are temples of the Holy Spirit. Our lives are not ours to shape in the image of the world around us. We have been called out. We have been set apart.

The world will continue offering what feels good to the senses, but God calls us into what is true. He calls us to remain alert, grounded, and unmoved by cultural drift.

The more we renew our minds, the stronger our identity becomes. We stop blending in. We start standing firm. And we live with the steady, quiet confidence of those who know exactly where they belong.

Reflection

Ask yourself:

1. Where am I slowly conforming?

2. Are there areas where the world's influence is shaping me more than the Word of God?

3. What daily rhythms can help me renew my mind and stay aligned with truth?

Scripture Meditation

Take time to read and reflect on each of these verses. Invite the Holy Spirit to speak to you through them.

- **Romans 12:2** — *"Do not be conformed to this world, but be transformed by the renewing of your mind, that you may prove what is that good and acceptable and perfect will of God."*

- **Daniel 1:8** — *"Daniel purposed in his heart that he would not defile himself with the portion of the king's delicacies..."*

- **Colossians 4:6** — *"Let your conversation be always full of grace, seasoned with salt, so that you may know how to answer everyone."*

Chapter Ten

Total Surrender

Mark 12:30 — *"And you shall love the Lord your God with all your heart, with all your soul, with all your mind, and with all your strength."*

Jesus commands us to love the Lord our God with all our heart, soul, mind and strength. With this command He invites us into a complete love for God by naming each part of our being, our heart, soul, mind, and strength. He did this because these are often the areas of life that drift away from Him. These parts of us do not naturally move toward obedience or surrender. They must be given to God intentionally.

The **heart** is often filled with emotions, desires, and motives that compete with the will of God. In **Jeremiah 17:9**, Scripture says, *"The heart is deceitful above all things, and desperately wicked; who can know it?"* When we love God with all our heart, we invite Him to cleanse our hidden motives and transform our desires. We choose to give Him full access to the core of our emotional and spiritual life.

The **soul** is the seat of our will. It often seeks to operate independently. Many choices are made in the soul that reflect a desire to control our own path. But **Proverbs 14:12** reminds us, *"There is a way that seems right to a man, but its end is the way of death."* Surrendering the soul to God means placing every decision, desire, and direction under His leadership.

The **mind** is where thoughts form, decisions take shape, and justifications are created. This is where pride, fear, and doubt often speak the loudest. **Romans 8:7** tells us, *"The mind governed by the flesh is hostile to God; it does not submit to God's law, nor can it do so."* When we love God with all our mind, we allow Him to renew our thoughts with His truth. We choose to think according to the Word rather than emotions, culture, or convenience.

Our **strength** represents effort, ability, and personal drive. Many people attempt to live for God through willpower alone. But **1 Samuel 2:9** says, *"By strength shall no man prevail,"* and **Zechariah 4:6** reminds us, *"Not by might nor by power, but by My Spirit,"* says the Lord of hosts. Loving God with all our strength means offering our abilities to Him and relying on His Spirit to carry us through every challenge.

Loving God in this way requires full surrender. This kind of love is not based on convenience or emotional highs. It is a daily posture of the heart that says, "God, I cannot do this without You." The moment we believe we can handle life apart from Him, we begin to drift. For this reason, **1 Corinthians 10:12** gives a stern reminder: *"Therefore let him who thinks he stands take heed lest he fall."*

There is great wisdom in the way Jesus phrased this command. He did not leave anything out. Our heart, soul, mind, and strength must all come under His Lordship. If even one part remains untouched by His presence, it becomes a place where spiritual compromise can begin. Every area must be surrendered so that God can fully dwell in us and through us.

Loving God completely is a way of living. It is a continual invitation for the Holy Spirit to fill and lead every area of our lives. God is not asking for perfection. He is asking for our devotion. He wants a heart that is willing to yield again and again.

Romans 12:1 says, *"I beseech you therefore, brethren, by the mercies of God, that you present your bodies a living sacrifice, holy, acceptable to God, which is your reasonable service."*

Reflection

Ask yourself:

1. Which part of you (heart, soul, mind, or strength) has been the hardest to surrender?

2. What does it look like to love God with your mind in your everyday life?

3. Have you been relying on your own strength? What would change if you invited the Holy Spirit to take over?

4. What is one step you can take today to bring your whole self under the leadership of Christ?

Scripture Meditation

Take time to read and reflect on each of these verses. Invite the Holy Spirit to speak to you through them.

- **Mark 12:30** — *"And you shall love the Lord your God with all your heart, with all your soul, with all your mind, and with all your strength."*

- **Jeremiah 17:9** — *"The heart is deceitful above all things, and desperately wicked; who can know it?"*

- **Proverbs 14:12** — *"There is a way that seems right to a man, but its end is the way of death."*

- **Romans 8:7** — *"The mind governed by the flesh is hostile to God; it does not submit to God's law, nor can it do so."*

- **1 Samuel 2:9** — *"By strength shall no man prevail."*

- **Zechariah 4:6** — *"Not by might nor by power, but by My Spirit," says the Lord of hosts.*

- **1 Corinthians 10:12** — *"Therefore let him who thinks he stands take heed lest he fall."*

- **Romans 12:1** — *"I beseech you therefore, brethren, by the mercies of God, that you present your bodies a living sacrifice, holy, acceptable to God, which is your reasonable service."*

About the author

About the Author

Ejiro Obayomi is a devoted wife, loving mother of three, ministry leader, and worship leader with a deep passion for intimacy with God and truth rooted in His Word. She lives in Gilbert, Arizona, where she also works professionally as a leader in a consulting firm. Whether she is guiding others in ministry, nurturing her family, or navigating the workplace, Ejiro strives to walk closely with the Lord in every season of life.

Though she never considered herself a writer, in recent years the Lord began to stir something new within her, speaking to her heart and granting fresh insights into the timeless truths of Scripture. As He faithfully revealed His heart, He also gently led her to write down what He was saying. What began as quiet moments with God turned into pages of encouragement, truth, and purpose.

Outside of writing and ministry, Ejiro enjoys singing and spending quality time with her family, whether through everyday moments at home or adventures that create lasting memories. *Knowing God in the Quiet* is her first book, born out of a desire to help others rediscover their identity in Christ and learn what it means to truly dwell in Him.

www.ingramcontent.com/pod-product-compliance
Lightning Source LLC
Chambersburg PA
CBHW070355130626
46556CB00007B/3173